Issued in print and electronic formats.
ISBN 978-1-7390527-1-3 (hardcover)
ISBN 978-1-7390527-2-0 (paperback)
ISBN 978-1-7390527-0-6 (ebook)

Cover Design: Jessica Schultz, Sweet Simple Collabs

Editor: Josephine LoRe

Photos: Gale Family archives except where noted.

Photos on pages 3 and 133 are courtesy of Greg Turlock, Greg Turlock Creative

Thank you to everyone who has contributed in any way to the production of this collection!

L'Opacité

A collection of poems
Une collection de poésie

Lynn Gale

For JP
Who loves me anyway
MLDG

Author's Note:

This collection contains poetry born from memories and experiences in my life.

While they are personal and filtered through the lenses of time, my hope is that they are also relatable to others who may have experienced some of same things I did growing up.

Isolation, alcoholism, dysfunction, feelings of not fitting in, or not being enough, feeling lost, confused, lonely, or unloved—these are emotions felt by many people universally.

It's hard to bare my soul and put my words out there, but it's even harder to keep them cloistered within.

I found peace in the writing of these poems and I hope that you find a small piece of connection, understanding, and solace while reading them.

They are my truth.

With love and gratitude,
Lynn

P.S. I would love to know if any of the poetry speaks to you. Feel free to reach out to me at www.lynngalewriter.com.

Index of Poetry

What Came Next
Open and Shut
Mon Centre (Center)
Âme Perdue (Lost Soul)
Lent
Peur de Tomber (Fear of Falling)
Christmas Dinner at the Hotel Frontenac
Désolée (Sorry)
Recommencer (Restart)

Closer to Now
Soulmate
Retourner à la lumière (Return to the Light)
Heartbeats
Wildcard
Soi (Self)
Uninvited
Baggage
Le Vide (The Void)
Dream Weaver
Threads *(Les Fils)*

Now
Finding Grace
Out of Sync
Precautions
Train Wreck
Seeing Clearly *(Voir Clairement)*
Waiting to Say Goodbye
Magic Then and Now
Luminosity *(Luminosité)*
L'Opacité (Opacity)

The Beginning

Wild Thing
Créature Sauvage

Giggling on sands of Côte d'Azur,
my little toes splash in warm water while
short curls bounce,
looking exotic and wild and free.

This child is a stranger to me.
Je suis un étrangère.

Sieste
Naptime

After falling asleep under the piano
at kindergarten
my mother explained
"Big girls don't nap"
which is strange
because yesterday
at home
I napped
and
it was okay.

J'ai pas compris.

Les Enfants
The Children

new baby
I got to name
who then replaced me   forever
in my parents' hearts

not the boy they wanted
the brother born too soon
weak lungs   they said
he won't survive

 (he didn't)

a new little girl
and my light faded*   forever
in my parents' eyes
please be quiet, child   they said

  the baby is sleeping

  *Jealousy is interchangeable with envy, the fourth
  deadly sin.

La Lumière
The Light

New little brother
cuddled on my lap
our sister at my side

cold baby feet
warm toddler breath

our dreams simple then
hearts longing for love

We had that in common

Home

Cookie cutter houses

not the good kind
that made cookies with icing and sprinkles

but the kind
that made undecorated day-old varieties.

PMQs we called them.*

We shared a sense of security
not from boundaries
but from a lack of knowing

and usually bad things didn't happen

at least

not where we could see them.

Permanent Married Quarters

Caged

A high wire fence
surrounded the air force base
to keep us in
to keep them out

(whoever *they* were)

A veritable zoo of oddities
for the rest of the world
to observe
and mock

Sink, Sank, Sunk

I failed Tadpoles in swimming
(who fails Tadpoles???)
and had to receive my participation award
in slippers and faded yellow pjs

Mom forgot about the swim-up ceremony
Dad couldn't be bothered
to remind me to change
into real clothes

After all,
let's face it
I didn't pass
so what did it matter?

Hard to breathe under water...

First Communion

I wore knee-socks, not even pure white

    sandals worn and faded

While my best friend had ankle socks, satin bows

    black patent Mary Janes

Envy is the fourth deadly sin.

A mortal sin as it is directly opposed to the virtue of charity which requires us to rejoice in the good fortune of others. Source: Faith-fi.com

Wandering

I spent a lot of time

outside

climbing trees

in the woods

behind our house   alone

I broke my glasses

once

craving attention

from the people

inside our house

I got taped glasses

instead

and

a reprimand

for being clumsy

as broken

on the outside

as I was

on the inside

of our house   alone

Hello/Goodbye

Bonjour/Au Revoir

Growing up on an air force base

Slightly farther away than *Where the hell is that*

But not as far as *That sounds nice*

Was like wearing a Scarlet A

We were somehow less

always ashamed

Good Enough

My Brownie uniform
handed down from a neighbour
slightly tight, multi-washed with obvious lines
where numerous hems had been let down.

The Brownie Promise
said 'Do your best'.
Hard to do
for when I bent over
I couldn't breathe.

Piégée

Trapped

Locked in a locker

at the rec centre once

I was eight

Everyone went home and

if the Chimo lounge lady hadn't needed to pee

I would probably be there still

Got home

Dad making Kraft dinner

(Mom in the hospital having our baby brother)

He saw my hands, scraped and raw

from pounding the inside of the metal locker door

my face, red from screaming

Help me

He asked what I'd been doing

and I was going to tell him

then my sister cried and he had to go

and he never asked again

The ache in my throat

not just from screaming

Hear me

Picasso

My sister and I shared a room
our brother had his own because
he was the only boy

I had a pulldown-shelf secretary desk
I dreamed of being an artist at that desk
and when I saw the ad
I carefully drew the face and mailed it in

A letter came back saying
that at age ten
I was too young to take the course
sorry

I met a girl at the lake that summer
who could draw people
eyes and mouths that saw and spoke
and I was thankful that the artist people
had crushed my dream

before she did

Façade
False Face

Dad drank a lot.

Mom did too but more

sporadic and determined.

Dad drank every day.

Mom would have me call the bar and ask if he was there.

If he was, I asked why he wasn't at home.

He would hang up and Mom would get madder.

He was the life of the party

and everyone loved him.

Our house party central.

We had to stay in our rooms.

We only had one bathroom

and it was downstairs

When I went down to pee

he'd drag me into the party

drunken hugs all around

then push me back to the bottom of the stairs

hissing, *Get back to bed now.*

Remembering

Waiting, under covers, breath held

for the moment but when it arrives,

caught unawares.

The crash, muffled curses

inevitable ensuing fight.

I shiver

not from cold.

The soft sound of crying

permeates the protective armour of my quilt.

I peek with one eye, see my sister

pale, teary, one arm grasping a teddy that

has seen better days yet still offering some

measure of comfort to a small child;

humans not as reliable.

I raise the sheet and she slides in, cold toes against my

legs, snuggling like a caterpillar in a cocoon.

Waiting.

A final slam precedes a return to silence.

Sometimes quiet more frightening than noise;

we must lie still

just in case.

I feel the silk of my sister's hair under my chin and

smell the apple shampoo my mother found in that corner

drugstore where the pharmacist pats our heads

and sadly smiles.

My sister slips back to sleep;

Breathing even and deep

while I dream of homes where conversations are not

punctuated with anger and hostility even when we all

behave as we should

and try to be good;

Good never enough.

The Middle Bit

Sway Bar

I dreamed of being average, ordinary

but

seemed to flounder on the bottom edge of okay

unless

I leaned into the center

of

What the hell are you doing now?

Vérité
Alone

I lived in my head and my books

read and dreamed

of other families who lived in peace.

Reality blended into fiction

with momentary gaps

where I couldn't tell real from unreal.

Lying

lines blurred

edges darkened

memory blanked.

I couldn't really tell

the difference.

If there was one.

Hello David Cassidy

I memorized every line
in *Tiger Beat,*
the gospel according to David.

There'd been that one guy
in grade seven
long gorgeous hair
who turned and glared when
he caught my stare.

That was different.
This was real.

David would love me back
because I was a fan
and he loved his fans.

It said so in *Tiger Beat.*

**Tiger Beat: American magazine founded in 1965 featuring teen
idol gossip.*

The Cottage

Every summer we went to visit

Manitoba cousins

Cottage screens covered

in layers of silverfish

Inside bathroom out of bounds

(to us)

We were forced to use the toilet in our trailer parked

like a pimple on the front garden

Barbed conversations

Arrows that struck

Smiles without kindness or humour

Judged and tolerated

Found wanting

Red River Jamboree

The last day of grade eight

I wore a pair of white GWGs

and a faux–suede fringed long vest

    maxi length

I thought I was pretty cool

until an odd sensation of

moisture warmed one ankle

    blood soaking the hem of my jeans

    like I'd been shot in the leg

I tied the vest around my waist using the long fringes

power-walked home where I put the

no-longer white pants in the bathtub

to soak

    Cold water for blood, right?

I tossed the Tampax box away in disgust

the river was strong and resisted

any efforts at reconciliation

    The pants joined the tampons in disgrace

in the garbage behind the garage

The ring on the tub pink for days

Karma

After I called Steve John too many times
he cottoned on and we had a talk

Went with John to grade nine grad
in a pink satin formal gown borrowed
from the sister of one of my friends

I felt like a princess until
halfway through the evening
the hem fell down
 (I had hemmed it myself)

John met the sister
of another friend
spent the evening with her

He had to walk me home
even though he said he had to pee
(but really wanted to stay and talk to the other girl)

the dress dragged through dirt
and ruined

Sgt's Mess

Kitchen help

Meant peeling more potatoes than

I'd ever seen in my life.

Then serving supper to those

Whose idea of an appetizer

Was a drink (or two) before eating.

Leers and laughter

Mixed with booze breath and melting butter.

Coming out after shift

To find someone waiting by my mom's car

The kitchen supervisor driving away

Leaving me with a drunken man

Who thought I too was on the menu.

Finally getting away

Asked next shift why she had left me

And told

I thought you wanted it that way.

I was sixteen.

A different kind of mess.

Shooting Stars

Needles were a thing

and getting high something you did.

There was a guy

who could get you what you wanted.

My friend said yes and went for a ride

then got lost in the stars.

I called her mom to come and find her.

My friend was saved

but our friendship lost.

Good friends don't let friends

almost die

even if the stars they are shooting for

are in a galaxy of their own making.

Northern Lights

Aurora borealis

most beautiful when it's cold and clear

and dark

Colours dance and make you believe

anything is possible

The back of a snowmobile at forty below colder

than you can imagine

but magic in the sky makes you forget

everything

until you realize the crackle in the air

is not the music of the lights

but ice on the lake

beneath you

as it bends, bows, and fractures

in a dance of its own

Pearls

There were good times too

with laughter and love

moments captured and cherished

I mean there had to be, right?

fragile and fleeing

all the more precious

I wish there were more

so I could string them

like pearls

shimmering in light

a fabulous necklace

that would

adorn and caress

rather than

strangle and choke

Scar Tissue

You are just like him

she'd rasp in anger

born of frustration

words cut deep

and left a mark

that to this day

my soul can see

and even

knowing why

and understanding

her pain

can't erase

jagged edges

Collapse

Hard to give love
when none was known
difficult to accept

that's just the way it was

no remorse
no excuses
just a shrug and a nod

Blood may bind
but ties are loose

glue is weak
structure shaky
without a solid foundation

What Came Next

Open and Shut

I wanted to be a teacher

Signed up for the courses I would need

Block one Psychology

Block two English

In high school, teachers loved my work

but at university it was less than acceptable

I wanted to ask what I needed to do

but my throat closed

Words shriveled and died

before they hit the air

Voice stifled, feet stilled

As the door closed

I turned to ash

and disappeared

Mon Centre
Center

I spent years

trying to be

what I thought I should be

to make it okay

wanting to please

to be part of something

of anything

always on the edge

or just outside the door

losing myself

to find love

any love

any acceptance

anywhere

that I could belong

it didn't work

I kept getting

more and more lost

and farther away

from my center

Âme Perdue
Lost Soul

wanted to get away

and when I did

all I felt was lonely

a life to start anew

fresh beginning, no past

but I lost the map

        I drive in circles

        missing my exit

        every

        single

        time

Lent

grey

outside and in

gorgeous dress doing nothing

to soothe or pierce

the dismal gloom

the church

the statues

draped for Lent

they hide from my shame

I want to make it right

whispers say *C'est trop tard*

too late, choices made

organ music starts

parish stands, straight-backed

murmurs drift

collective breaths

hold

pause

wait

I step   forward

Peur de Tomber
Fear of Falling

I could have sat

for hours

beside rushing waters

    the sound

    the sight

    the rush of power

        majestic and true

        rushing towards the edge

        without fear

            spilling over

            steadfast in their journey

            to what lay below

                determined yet driven

                free and joyful

                    being and doing

                    what comes naturally

                    in spite of the rocks below

                    why can't I

Christmas Dinner at the Hotel Frontenac

silence can be torture

when used to shut you out

a scream without sound

is still a scream

it burrows deep

emerges other ways

to make itself heard

but you never heard

and I couldn't find the way

to make you listen

even when I whispered

les bouchées du Père Noël en chocolat

were good though

the croissants

to die for

Désolée
Sorry

There is no going back

no do-overs

no second chances

to make it right

or make it last

there is only now and going forward

  every breath a gift

    a hope

        that this time will be better

            than before

Recommencer

Restart

I was used to starting over

every few years

my own Advance to Go

a way to shove old hurts

beneath the bed

taped in cardboard boxes

and forgotten

a way to cope

my only way

when that was no longer an option

I had to fight

or lose my place in line

I chose to stay

and slowly the boxes

under the bed

disintegrated

into dust

Closer

to

Now

Soulmate

I should have known

when I met you

that you were

the one for me

I knew you

yet I resisted

in spite of that

we became us

in the end

or maybe it was the beginning

it doesn't matter

you see me

no one ever has

or ever will

and I

I see you too

Retourner à la Lumière
Return to the Light

Outside on the earth

with our families and friends

pledging our troth

(such an old-fashioned word)

under a deep blue Alberta sky

this is how it should have been

before

this is how it was meant to be

before

I'm sorry it took me

so long to hear the

truth of my heart

and the answering

whisper of yours

Heartbeats

When I carried our babies
and listened to their hearts beat
for the very first time
it was a music my body already
knew

the sensation of the knowing
was unlike anything I'd
ever felt before

I'd forgotten
that my own heart
also beats
a rhythm of its own
music of my soul

music I already knew
but had never heard
before

until that moment

Wildcard

friends and family I hold dear

like diamonds in the sun

stars in a banner of darkness

goodbye doesn't dull

the light or the memories

the ache remains

as my heart remembers

we think we have all the time in the world

to be what we want to be

do what we want to do

but the hand that deals the card

doesn't have to draw

from the right side of the deck

and the joker

is always wild

Soi

Self

finding self

is not as clear and easy

as it may sound

self doesn't have all the answers

but usually more questions

we are connected in this world

to the universe

to each other

to ourselves

yet the more we look inside

the more we see

the answers

don't matter

anyway

Uninvited

unintended

unexpected

wounds that never heal

fragments

repositioned

remnants

reattached

scars

invisible

continue to ache

especially when it rains

Baggage

Sometimes

burdens we carry are not our own

but over time

they mingle with our

DNA

becoming

part of who we are

C'est très bon de savoir quand dire

"The buck stops here and rest our backs"

Le Vide
The Void

craving stillness

deep inside

to calm

to ground

to balance

found it in my breath

a space

carved just

for me

from me

body

mind

soul together

like strangers

on a train

finally

saying hello

Dream Weaver

fragments

      remnants

my past

      space between

each strand

      my breath

        space to breathe

space to speak

        space to listen

space to dream

      my dreams

imperfect stitches

        sewn to

my soul

        thread

fragments

      weaving

        dreams

Threads
Les Fils

Mémère

St. Boniface Cathedral

Rivière Rouge

Assiniboine Park

Provencher Bridge

Formica table

Taché Avenue

Clawfoot bathtub

Another world that came before

A slender *fil* between us

Un petit aperçu du passé

Gone but not forgotten

Jamais oublié

Now

Finding Grace

Hard to concentrate on joy

when weighted down by a leaden heart

yet at the end of the day

we are built to survive

despite sadness

   despite loss

      despite grief

this prevents our extinction

doesn't mean what happens is okay

only means when we accept what is, as it is

we can move on with grace

Out of Sync

Who sets the norm, I wonder?

Who gives who (whom?) the right to decide what is in and what is out?

If we are each the individuals we like to think we are, doesn't that make more of us than them (the invisible who/ whom)?

    Out of step,

        half a dance move behind,

            or several swim-lengths ahead.

Do I slow down, or speed up?

Where and what is the ultimate answer?

Do I teach my children to fit in, or be themselves?

What if being themselves makes them too different?

Worse yet, what if it makes them too much the same?

    When we're cut, we bleed

        And that blood is red

            For each and every one of us

                Any differences unseen by the naked eye.

underneath

    we are all in sync

        so

            why can't we be

                on the outside too?

Precautions

Warning, warning!

Avoid coffee and sunlight

Together, I wonder?

What if I avoided only one at a time?

Tea and sunlight a winning combination

Coffee and rain work well in a pinch

Pills in my hand. I pause, frozen in time

while I mull the consequences of my next step.

The sunscreen on the shelf *(50)* mocks me

I inhale the fragrant smell

of Kona macadamia nut coffee

from Greenwell Farms in Hawaii

making its way through my Nespresso

a fitting end to a journey of a few thousand miles.

Warm sun, hot coffee

memories of morning air heavy with gardenia

play with my mind as I ponder

whether to take the pills to ease my pain

or drink the coffee in the sun to soothe my soul.

Train Wreck

When we first moved to this town

a young woman was hit by a train

just a hundred or so meters from our backyard.

Not right behind our house but a few blocks west

the edgy squeal of brakes resonating along the track

echoing the moonlit night for miles.

I imagine the frantic engineer applying

maximum load of force, plus more,

with all his might

as she walked the tracks.

Towards home?

Away?

Earbuds dulling the sound of the approach

although surely her feet could feel the rhythm

in the iron rails as it got closer

or maybe she did feel it but chose to stay.

Too late to stop the train.

Seeing Clearly
Voir Clairement

I saw some cool steampunk glasses

endless arms, lenses of all colors

and abilities.

Each one designed to see

where usually eyes could not.

Into souls.

    Into dreams.

        Into fears.

Into someone's very essence.

Seeing clearly

what no one else did

through eyes unaided

by magic

and illusion.

Waiting to Say Goodbye

my whole life it felt like you were waiting waiting for things to get better waiting to finish your degree waiting for dad to come home you unhappy while you waited living in a state of grey disengaging retreating into your own world you called it reading but it was really escaping your everyday for as long as I remember I was never enough

the kids you taught dearer to you, smarter, brighter I a disappointment until the end and even then I wasn't sure nothing ever good—it was always too something or not something enough your hugs hollow your praise given only for achievement never for effort I thought our kids would make a difference but they didn't you focused on other people's kids they were more interesting

I think you might have tried to care but it didn't stick I don't think you ever felt enough for yourself either you were angry something in you hardened to the world denied a loving childhood you knew of no other way to parent so we grew but didn't flourish shells—pretend people who didn't know how to be and still you waited

we tried to love you your voice spoke the words I love you but only when we did something for you never for just being us but how could we blame you you our mother instead we blamed ourselves the circle complete as we never thought we were enough either but didn't know how to fix it and now you are gone and I thought I would feel peace but I can only think of how I failed you right to the end you waited

you waited for us to notice what you needed as you grew frail and we tried but it was never enough and you finally had to stop eating to get your way I'd like to think we gave you comfort and a gentle place for you to pass holding the soft red stuffed moose a beacon waiting for peace and even then there was a moment when I wondered if this was what you truly wanted or If you were just tired of waiting I wish I knew so I could make it right for you I'm sorry Mom that we never said a proper goodbye before or after we tried and you deserved a better

adieu

Mémère

September 5, 1930—December 18, 2015

Magic Then and Now

Children believe in magic
until they don't.

When you were small, your toes
cracked and split and made you cry with pain.
You believed the white salve I gently applied
was magic toe cream
because I said it was.

As you got older
you realized it wasn't magic
merely medicinal and effective.

But I still remember the wonder
on your face
when the magic happened
and your toes didn't hurt.

Luminosity
Luminosité

Have you ever noticed

how much brighter the world appears

when you are happy?

How joy adds depth and colour

that only sadness can take away.

Grief comes in many shades of grey

roughened by tear-filled eyes

worn and faded by hands clenching

and unclenching.

Light and dark swirl

through colours thick and rich

the deepest black

the clearest white

swirling and settling

into

a luminosity custom-built

by you.

L'Opacité
Opacity

J'adore la langue française

    (English can be so discordant)

Est-ce que je veux être mémère

    or just gramma?

Both are me

    (Les deux sont moi)

       Les deux sont moi

Printed in the USA
CPSIA information can be obtained
at www.ICGtesting.com
LVHW092030191123
764361LV00004BA/460